Peace of Heart in All Things

Brother Roger is the founder of the Taizé Community. It was in 1940 that he settled in the French village of Taizé. Praying three times a day, he gave shelter to political refugees, notably Jews, and gathered them around him a group of men from different Christian traditions who committed themselves to community life and to celibacy.

There are now 100 brothers from across the world, some of them living in situations of great poverty and division. Since 1957, Taizé has welcomed ever-increasing numbers of young adults in weekly meetings throughout the year. Through the daily prayer and by returning to the roots of faith with others from across the globe, they seek meaning in their lives. At the end of each year, Taizé prepares a vast meeting for up to 100,000 young people in one of the major cities in Europe. Similar gatherings are held on the other continents.

G-4649

PEACE of HEART IN ALL THINGS

Meditations for Each Day of the Year

Brother Roger

GIA Publications, Inc.
Chicago

Library of Congress Cataloging-in-Publication Data
Roger, frère, 1915–
    Peace of heart in all things : meditations for each day of the
    year / Brother Roger.
        p. cm.
    Includes bibliographical references.
    ISBN 0-941050-96-3 (alk. paper)
        1. Peace of mind—Religious aspects—Christianity—Meditations.
    2. Devotional calendars. I. Title
    BV4908.5.R57 1996
    242'.2—dc21   96-53041
                                                                CIP

© 1996 Ateliers et Presses de Taizé
71250 The Taizé Community, France
English translation © 1995 Ateliers et Presses de Taizé
Published and distributed in North America exlusively by
GIA Publications, Inc.
7404 S. Mason Ave., Chicago, IL 60638

ISNB: 0-941050-96-3

CONTENTS

ABOUT THIS BOOK

This book offers a brief meditation for each day of the year. These short texts attempt to express realities which we can return to, day after day, our whole life long.

This book also contains a hundred or so prayers, printed in italics. They are often expressed in the first person plural. When they are used for personal meditation, the *we* naturally becomes *I*.

The texts for Holy Week and Pentecost have been placed between the months of March and April, since the dates change every year.

At the end of the book can be found a number of Bible passages dealing with trust and peace of heart.

PREFACE

This book was written for those who aspire to maintain peace of heart in all things, living in joy, simplicity, and mercy.

With very little, sometimes with just a few words, it is possible over time to forge our inner selves.

If our days seem to hold no future, we withdraw and become closed up within ourselves.

When disenchantment gains the upper hand and our steps grow heavy, when a fine human hope or, still more, hope in God vanishes from our life, then our innermost heart becomes frozen.

Peace of heart can be welcomed or neglected. When the way forward becomes obscured by events, it is more indispensable than ever.

I have written these pages as much for myself as for those who will read them.

Jesus, be our peace. You never want us to experience the upheavals of spiritual desolation. When we realize that everything depends upon our trusting in your love, then we listen to your call: By the Holy Spirit make yourself a heart determined to welcome everything in the radiance of praise.

January

January 1

Whoever is on a journey towards God goes from one beginning to another beginning. Will you be among those who dare to tell themselves: "Begin again! Leave discouragement behind! Let your soul live!"

January 2

Although there may well be shocks and even upheavals in our lives, Jesus the Christ is there. He will always say to us: "Even when you are going through the harshest trial, I am present underneath your despair. . . . And I am also there deep within your hope."

January 3

Jesus, light of our hearts, since you rose from the dead, you have never stopped coming to us. Whatever point we may be at, you are always waiting for us. And you tell us: "Come to me, you who are overburdened, and you will find relief."[1]

January 4

For those who discover Saint John, the most captivating thing is to glimpse this radiant insight: "God is love[2] . . . and Christ did not come to earth to judge the world, but so that, through him, the Risen Lord, every human being might be saved and reconciled."[3]

January 5

Alleviating human suffering is at the heart of the Gospel. When we allay other people's trials, we do it for Christ himself; he is the one we encounter. "Whatever you do for the least of my brothers and sisters," he says, "you do for me."[4]

January 6

Even if you seem to have very little faith, will you prepare yourself to welcome a Gospel light? "It shines in the darkness and the darkness was unable to put it out."[5]

January 7

God of every human being, you never force our heart, but you place your peaceful light within each one of us. With that light shining upon them, our failures and our joys can find meaning in you.

January 8

There are countries where visible "homes for the dying" are to be found. In Western civilization, in addition, there are "homes for the dying" that are invisible. Children and young people there are marked for life because they have been abandoned; they are affected down to their very depths by broken relationships, by lack of affection. Their hearts are sometimes dying of loneliness. They feel as if they are on an ocean with no lighthouse. Some even reach the point of losing all desire to live. Are not situations of human abandonment one of the deepest traumas of our time?

9

January 9

In all things peace of heart, serene joy. Centuries before Christ, a believer had already prayed with these words: "In God alone my soul finds rest, my hope comes from him; God alone is an unshakable support."[6] And in the Gospel, Christ gives us this assurance: "Peace is my gift to you; I leave you my peace. Do not let your hearts be troubled or afraid."[7]

January 10

Six centuries after Christ a Christian thinker, Isaac of Nineveh, wrote these words of fire: "All God can do is give his love." Those who understand this luminous reality begin to ask themselves: How can I communicate such a solid hope?

January 11

Breath of Christ's loving, Holy Spirit, in the depths of our soul you set faith. It is like a surge of trusting, repeated countless times over in the course of our life. It can only be a simple act of trust, so simple that everyone can welcome it.

January 12

To let ourselves be refreshed by living water welling up inside us, it is good to go off for a few days in silence and peace.

Long ago Elijah, the believer, set out in search of a place where he could listen to God. He climbed a mountain in the wilderness. A hurricane arose, the earth began to shake, a conflagration broke out. Elijah knew that God was not in these outbursts of nature. God is never the author of earthquakes or natural disasters.

Then everything became quiet and there was the murmur of a gentle breeze. Elijah covered his face. He had come to the realization that God's voice also made itself understood in a breath of silence.[8]

January 13

Some brothers of our community have been living in Bangladesh for many years, sharing the lives of the poorest people. One of them wrote, "After a cyclone, our neighbors asked us: Why all these misfortunes? Have we sinned against God so much?" What made their suffering worse was the secret fear of a punishment from God.

God never causes fear, anguish, or distress. He shares the suffering of those going through incomprehensible trials. And he enables us in our turn to alleviate the suffering of others. God wants neither wars, nor earthquakes, nor the violence of accidents. God is innocent of all this; God is innocence.

January 14

A luminous Gospel insight has come to light after remaining under the dust of the ages for a long time: even if the Risen Christ is unrecognized, he is present, "united to every human being without exception."[9]

January 15

God of all loving, you fill us with the freshness of the Gospel when a heart that trusts is at the beginning of everything.

January 16

Happy are those who can make this prayer their own: Christ, you see who I am. For me, not to hide anything in my heart from you is a necessity. You were a human being too. And when my inner self seems to be pulled in a thousand different directions, my thirsting heart reaches the point of praying: enable me to live a life rooted in you, Jesus the Christ; unify my desire and my thirst.

January 17

Where would we be today if certain women, men, young people, and also children had not arisen at moments when the human family seemed destined for the worst? They did not say: "Let things take their course!" Beyond the confrontations between persons, peoples, and spiritual families, they prepared a way of trusting. Their lives bear witness to the fact that human beings have not been created for hopelessness.

January 18

When tirelessly the Church listens, heals, and reconciles, it becomes what it is at its most luminous—a communion of love, of compassion, of consolation, a limpid reflection of the Risen Christ.

Never distant, never on the defensive, freed from all forms of severity, the Church can let the humble trusting of faith shine right into our human hearts.

January 19

Jesus our joy, by your continual presence within us, you lead us to give our life. Even if we forget you, your love remains, and you send your Holy Spirit upon us.

January 20

From the time of the apostles, the Virgin Mary, and the first believers, there has been a call to live in great simplicity and to share. One of the pure joys of the Gospel is to go further and further toward a simplicity of heart that leads to a simplicity of living.

January 21

Simplifying never means choosing an ice-cold austerity, without kindheartedness, filled with judgments upon those who do not take the same road. If simplicity of life became equated with moroseness, how could it lead us to the Gospel? The spirit of simplicity shines through in signs of serene joy, and also in cheerfulness of heart. Simplifying invites us to arrange what little we have in creation's simple beauty.

January 22

With almost nothing, above all through the gift of our lives, the Risen Christ desires that both fire and Spirit be made perceptible in us.[10]

However poor we may be, let us not quench the fire, let us not quench the Spirit.[11] In them the wonder of a love bursts into flame. And the humble trusting of faith is communicated like fire spreading from one person to the next.

January 23

Jesus our trust, your Gospel brings with it such a fine hope that we would like to give ourselves to the very end in order to follow you. And irresistibly the question arises: Where is the source of our joy? It is found in peace and in a heart overflowing with infinite goodness.

January 24

One day in Taizé a child said, "My father left us. I never see him, but I still love him and at night I pray for him." Without realizing it, that child was living the miracle of kindheartedness.

January 25

Whoever seeks reconciliation with a simple heart is able to pass through rock-hard situations like the water of a stream which, in early springtime, makes its way through the still frozen ground.

January 26

An Orthodox theologian from Bucharest, Father Staniloae, who had been in prison for his beliefs, wrote words which are so essential that we would like to know them by heart:

> I looked for God in the human beings of my village, then in books and in ideas. But that brought me neither peace nor love. One day, while reading the Church Fathers, I discovered that it was actually possible to encounter God through prayer. I gradually realized that God was close to me, that he loved me, and that, filled by his love, my heart opened to others. I realized that love was a communion, with God and with others. And without that communion, everything is only sadness and desolation.

January 27

Holy Spirit, mystery of a presence, you bathe us in unfailing kindness. It allows a life of humble trusting to blossom in us. . . . And our hearts become lighter.

January 28

Self-mastery out of love for others keeps us alert. This may be the price we pay for peace of heart, both for others and for ourselves: not letting ourselves be overcome by emotions or impressions that are so often magnified by the imagination.

January 29

When darkness and doubts assail you, why not keep them at arm's length? Often they are only interludes of unbelief, nothing more. Why see yourself as dry ground? When his dew appears, the tears of the morning, a thirst is quenched in the desert of your soul.

January 30

Could there be a chasm of fears, doubts or loneliness inside us? Joy! Joy of the soul! The depths of worry in us call out to other depths,[12] the inexhaustible compassion of his love. And what a surprise: trust was at hand, and so often we were unaware of it.

January 31

Christ Jesus, when we think we are alone, you are there. If there seems to be doubt within us, that does not make you love us any the less. We would like to be daring enough to take risks on account of you, Christ. So we pay attention to your words: "Those who give their life for love of me will find it."[13]

February

February 1

Nothing is more beautiful than a face made transparent by a whole lifetime of sorrows and joys, of combats, and of inner peace.

February 2

When Mary and Joseph presented Jesus in the Temple, they only had two doves to offer.[1] Aren't we Christ's poor too, feeling our way forward as we search for him? And aren't Christ's eyes especially attentive to what is fragile in us?

February 3

God of peace, you do not want us to know relentless worry but rather a humble repentance of heart. It is like a surge of trusting that enables us to place our faults in you. And then, by the inner light of forgiveness, little by little we discover a peace of heart.

February 4

So many Christians find in prayer the courage to take on responsibilities. Rooting themselves in the very wellsprings of Christ, they run the risks of faith.

February 5

One day Saint Teresa of Avila and Saint John of the Cross came together for a meal. Grapes were brought in.

"I am not going to eat any," stated John of the Cross. "Too many people have none."

"I, on the contrary, will eat some," replied Teresa of Avila, "in order to praise God for these grapes."

February 6

Christ of compassion, through your Gospel we discover that measuring what we are or what we are not leads nowhere. What matters is the humble trusting of faith. By it we are led to glimpse the innocence of God and to understand that "All God can do is give his love."

February 7

Happy the person who, at grips with an uncomfortable situation, dares to say, "I am like a bird singing in a thorn bush."[2] Doesn't the Gospel invite us to welcome the Holy Spirit in that part of ourselves where our childhood heart is still to be found?

February 8

As you walk in Christ's footsteps, do not be surprised at his words: "Whoever puts his hand to the plow cannot look back."[3] He invites you to leave behind bitterness, regrets, all that corrodes eternity's yes. Could this yes become worn out? Will it no longer keep you awake your whole life long?

February 9

Could we think we have given up Christ? He never gives up on us. Do we feel we have abandoned him? He is present. That is something we never expected. That is more than we could ever hope for.

February 10

Jesus, joy of our hearts, ever since your resurrection, your light has been shining within us. Even if we were fragile and destitute, we could still tell you: We love you without having seen you,[4] and we would like to love you with our whole soul, with our whole heart.

February 11

When timidity keeps you from asking for forgiveness, why not dare to make a simple gesture that does not need words? Put out your hand so that the other person can make the sign of forgiveness in it, the sign of the cross.

February 12

Prayer enables us to discover where to find rest for our soul. And we are shown a reality hidden from human eyes: by his mysterious presence, Christ is always with us. And the heart, even when overwhelmed by trials, can begin to sing again: "Your compassion has visited me."

February 13

O Christ, you are united to every human being without exception. Still more, risen from the dead, you come to heal the secret wound of the soul. And for each person the gates of an infinite goodness of heart are opened. Through such a love, our lives change little by little.

February 14

In the years when wars followed one after the other in Southeast Asia, in Taizé we were deeply influenced by a man of God from Vietnam. He said this prayer standing in our midst, before returning home, where he soon met a violent death:

I am afraid of my fear,
I am afraid to leave you, Lord.
I am afraid of my fear,
I am afraid I will not hold out till the end.
Do not forget that I live for you.
Give me the grace to give you my entire life
And the love that will make me one with you.

February 15

Inconsistencies sometimes find their way into that communion of love which is the Body of Christ, his Church. They cause a lot of suffering. So then, are we going to run away from that communion? No, never. All we can do is to run towards it, from the ends of the earth if need be, and discern the miracle of a presence, the presence of the Risen Christ.

February 16

There is nothing naive about the spirit of childhood, about simplicity according to the Gospel. They are inseparable from discernment. They call for maturity and infinite courage. Far from being simplistic, they are steeped in clearsightedness.

February 17

Jesus our peace, by the Holy Spirit you always come to us. And in the deepest part of our soul, there is the wonder of a presence. Our prayer may be quite poor, but you pray within us.

February 18

Doubt can be corrosive. It can cast human beings down to the bottom of a well. But there is always a light still shining from above. Obscurity is not the dead of night; it is not pitch-darkness. It does not inundate the whole of our being. The light of Christ still penetrates it.

February 19

When we open the Gospel, this thought can come to us: Jesus' words are like a very old letter written to me in an unknown language. Since the author of these words is Christ, someone who loves me, I try to understand their meaning, and I am going to put into practice in my life the little I can grasp.

February 20

Holy Spirit, deep within us there is a longing, the longing to know inner freedom through you. This freedom is so essential for our lives: it opens the way to a springtime of the heart.

February 21

Children bring such happiness to our lives! Who can express adequately what some of them can communicate, to the point of being a reflection of the invisible communion? . . .

February 22

Some Eastern Christians are very attached to the prayer of the Name of Jesus. There are those for whom simply repeating the name Jesus expresses the fullness of a communion. Throughout the world, other Christians pray almost unceasingly with a few words: "Christ Jesus, let not my darkness speak to me; let me welcome your love." Or else they repeat that age-old prayer: "Let nothing trouble you, God alone is enough." Or again, they pray to Christ at every moment: "In you is peace of heart." And they find peace in their longing.

February 23

People who try to follow Christ by a yes for an entire lifetime are not unaware that there are fragilities within them. In days when trust seems to vanish, they call to mind these Gospel words: "Follow me and you will find rest for your heart."[5]

February 24

Savior of every life, you do not want inner anguish for anyone. And you come to shed light in us on the mystery of human suffering, to such an extent that you open the way to an intimacy with God.

February 25

When the heart is wounded or humiliated, it finds peace by entrusting to God, without waiting a single moment, those who have offended or mistreated it.

February 26

In our lives there are choices that come straight from the Gospel: forgiveness, reconciliation, or a struggle to remain faithful. Accomplished for the sake of Christ, these choices express to him our love.

February 27

Two centuries after Christ's death a believer wrote, "The calling God gives to Christians is so important that it is not possible for them to run away from it."[6] To run away from what? To run away from the responsibilities drawn from the wellsprings of the faith.

February 28

God of every human being, when we entrust ourselves to you in a spirit of thanksgiving, you lead us far from our hesitations. And you enable us to communicate to others a flame of hope by the lives we live.

February 29

Without forgiveness, without reconciliation, is there any future for a human being seeking fulfillment? And without reconciliation, what future is there for Christians?

March

March 1

When science and faith are seen as opposites, as if we had to choose one against the other, the depths of our being are affected. The effort to acquire qualifications can never be set in opposition to contemplative waiting on God.

March 2

How vigilant we must be not to stick any labels on anyone's forehead! Using expressions like "anguish," "pride," "jealousy" is not without consequences. Human beings so easily run the risk of looking for reasons, imaginary or not, to justify such judgments. Having a rigid image of another person can paralyze the whole evolution of their personality.

March 3

Christ Jesus, from the beginning you were in God.[1] When you came to live among human beings, you made the humble trusting of faith accessible. And the day is coming when we can say: I belong to Christ, I am Christ's.

March 4

Some Christians are utterly disconcerted when they hear that their faith is illusory, or that it is supposedly the projection of an unconsciously infantile attitude. Then doubt can creep into the soul. But there is nothing alarming about doubt. Inner freedom will open a way from hesitation towards trusting. The Gospel will always tell each one of us: "Seek, seek and you will find; do not let the fire in you go out."

March 5

Could there be a period of dryness in our life? Tirelessly Christ is seeking us. And we discover him as if for the first time. Even when he is rejected, he never refuses to remain alongside us.

March 6

With you, Risen Christ, we go forward from one discovery to another. As we try to find out what you want from us, our life opens up to the Holy Spirit. And he comes to bring to fulfillment in us things we did not even dare hope for.

March 7

Prayer does not always cause an outpouring of love for Christ. When fervor evaporates, there are times when this reality becomes apparent: the Risen Christ is not the one who went away; I am the one who is absent.

March 8

Even young children can experience trust in Christ. Go into a place of worship with a child, stand before an icon with him or her, and the life of that child will be warmed by the glow of an invisible presence. A flame has been kindled. Sooner or later it will burn in their heart of hearts.

March 9

Wishing to possess happiness for itself alone often causes it to vanish. Peace of heart and serene joy are offered to those who go to the point of giving their lives for love of Christ.

March 10

Living God, you bury our past in the heart of Christ and you are going to take care of our future.

March 11

The Gospel never calls us to moroseness. It never views human beings with pessimism. Just the opposite. It comes to awaken a peaceful joy.

March 12

There are people for whom God is so dazzling that they are blinded and consider themselves to be agnostics. What they know of God is above all his silence.

March 13

Peace of heart in all things. Our peace of heart communicates the gift of pacification to those around us. Peace of heart leads to serene joy. It is one of its sources.

March 14

Praying with you, Christ Jesus, the words that came to your lips on the cross, "Father, forgive them, they do not know what they are doing,"2 leads us to this other prayer: "Father, forgive me; sometimes it happens that I too hurt others without realizing it."

March 15

There is one thing we shall never fully understand: fragile as we are like vessels of clay, why did God call us to be bearers of Christ's hope? Because "the radiance comes from God, not from us."3

March 16

"All God can do is give his love." What God asks of us above all else is to surrender ourselves to him. And what a discovery! A fire burning in the soul, his compassion reawakens an inexhaustible goodness in our heart of hearts.

March 17

Holy Spirit, your love is a fire. In a communion with you, even when we seem to have received no answer to our prayers, that love has already accomplished something within us, and we may not even know how.

March 18

All who journey from one beginning to another in a life of communion with Jesus, the Christ, have no need to focus on their own progress or backsliding. By day and by night the Gospel seed, placed in the depths of their being, sprouts and grows.[4]

March 19

Does a Gospel joy leave our existence when we are affected by trials, illness, or bleak news from around the world?

To people at the extreme point of human suffering, a Gospel joy can be restored. It is comfort. And a reorientation of our being takes place; the Gospel comes to change our life.

March 20

Jesus our peace, you send your Holy Spirit upon us, as you did upon your disciples after your resurrection. It is like a fire that never says, "Enough!"[5]

March 21

Even the valley of tears can become a place of living springs.[6] And then we are free, able to look at people and things with poetry . . . free to glimpse already on this earth the dawning of a life that will never end.

March 22

When changes in society come faster and faster, the older generations, often living in isolation, can be confronted with situations that are not easy to deal with. They too need compassion, sometimes even consolation. How can we move forward without plunging the older generations into an abyss of worry at the same time?

March 23

When God's silences make their appearance, resting in him is already a way of reaching that oasis where he quenches our thirsts.

March 24

God of every human being, keep us from digging "cracked cisterns that do not hold the living water."[7] We want to entrust ourselves to you, surrendering to you our worries and our entire lives.

March 25

When we are faced with the Gospel call to say yes for our entire lifetime, sometimes the question arises: How can I remain faithful? The yes fascinates, and at the same time it can frighten. And we hesitate. But one day we are astonished to find ourselves on the road, walking in Christ's footsteps: the yes had been placed in the very depths of our being by the Holy Spirit. Then we begin to understand Mary's response: "May it be done to me according to your word."[8]

March 26

Deserts of the heart do exist. But perhaps there are fewer of them than we think! Isn't the Holy Spirit, the Comforter, present in each one of us?

March 27

Looking back to what has wounded us, lingering over our failures, paralyzes us right to the fibers of the soul. In new beginnings, the Holy Spirit accomplishes a miracle—he sets us free, he blots out the past, he leads us to love.

March 28

Holy Spirit, comforting Spirit, happy are they who turn to you over and over again! And when we entrust to you, even without words, our lives and those of others, our longings find a Gospel response.

March 29

Chase away fleeting cares like a child blowing on a dry leaf.

Don't cling to worries like a hand clutching the branch of a thorn bush; let go, and let Christ welcome you.[9]

March 30

Whatever point we may be at, the Risen Christ searches tirelessly for us. Do we hear him knocking at our door when he tells us: "Come, follow me"?[10]

March 31

Christ Jesus, when temptation urges us to abandon you, you pray within us. And you encourage us not to remain in darkness, but to live in your light.

Holy Week
and
Pentecost

Holy Thursday

The day before he was tortured on a cross, Jesus went off to pray in Gethsemane. He asks us just as he asked his disciples: "Will you stay with me to keep watch and pray?"[1]

Good Friday

When our eyes are fixed on the face of Jesus hanging on the cross, we would like to tell him: "Savior of every human being, you knew failure in your life. Overwhelmed by trials, you did not threaten anyone.[2] Following you can entail taking up our own cross.[3] And you carry it with us."[4]

Holy Saturday

Christ Jesus goes down to the lowest point of our human condition. Still more, he even goes to visit those who died without having known anything about him when they were on earth.[5]

Easter Sunday

Jesus our joy, with you we find forgiveness, the cool flowing waters. Thirsting for the realities of God, we recognize your presence as the Risen Lord. And like the almond tree that begins to blossom in the light of springtime, you make even the deserts of our soul burst into flower.

Pentecost Sunday

Jesus our peace, we know very little about praying but we remember your words: I will send you the Holy Spirit; he will be a source of comfort, remaining with you for ever.[6]

April

April 1

If Christ were not risen, he would not be present alongside us today. He would just be a remarkable personality in the history of humanity. It would not be possible to discover a communion in him, to share with him through prayer.

April 2

Joy and peace of heart are incomparable values for following Christ. Fear and worry can undermine the confident trusting of faith.

April 3

God our Father, in humble prayer we remember the words which one believer said to Jesus: "I believe, Lord, but come to help my lack of faith."[1] *When a portion of unbelief remains within us, your mercy upholds our faith.*

April 4

Whoever has experienced the approach of death in their youth senses that, even more than the body, it is the depths of the self that are first and foremost in need of healing. A childhood or youth fraught with trials can engender the boldness needed to run risks for the Gospel. Trust is at hand. . . .

April 5

It sometimes happens that we go so far as to question Christ Jesus: . . . But what is going on in me? Why these times when I grow weary in persevering? I am seeking you, so how can I linger over suggestions so foreign to the Gospel? Explain me to myself! . . .

April 6

When we pray, if we find that human language is almost incapable of expressing the depths of our being, there is no need to be alarmed. In a prayer steeped in silence, we rest in God— body, soul, and spirit.

April 7

Jesus, joy of our hearts, you remain alongside us like someone who is poor and also as the Risen Lord. You want to turn us into people who are fully alive, not lukewarm. And every time a distance opens up between ourselves and you, you invite us to follow you by remaining close to you.

April 8

On the evening of his resurrection, Jesus came up to two of his disciples who were going to the village of Emmaus. But they did not realize that the Risen Christ was walking alongside them.[2]

There are times in our life when we lose the awareness that, through the Holy Spirit, the Risen Christ is with us. Whether recognized or not, he is present, even when nothing seems to indicate it.

April 9

If we could only realize in the simplicity of faith that Christ, risen from the dead, is above all else communion. . . . He did not come to start a new religion, but to offer every human being this mystery of a communion in his Body, his Church.

April 10

Breath of Christ's loving, you enable us to be in communion with those who have gone before us, and they sometimes remain so close. They are already contemplating the invisible. You are preparing us, in their footsteps, to welcome a ray of your brightness.

April 11

How many men and women think they never do enough for those entrusted to them! And so they judge themselves. Could they even go so far as to forget the words of Saint John: "If our heart condemns us, God is greater than our heart"?[3]

April 12

Who will open their eyes to the anguish of the innocent?: children marked for life by broken relationships, by being abandoned, and also elderly people who are forced to live in unbearable loneliness. Who will run to join them?

April 13

God wants to make us living signs of his Christ. Will those entrusted to us discover in us reflections of the trusting of faith? But selflessness requires discretion, so that the burning flame of the Gospel be left to do its work.

April 14

Christ, you give everything; you give your life as well as your forgiveness; it will never go away. And we stammer our reply: You know that I love you, Christ,[4] perhaps not as I would like to, but I do love you.

April 15

Could not living the Easter mystery sometimes lead to discovering a serene joy even at the heart of trials? When there is intense suffering the heart can be broken, but it is not hardened.

April 16

When human beings grasp intuitively the vast beauty of things, there can be a sense in which that takes hold of them, however partially. Is not contemplation an inner disposition in which the whole being is caught up in the wonder of a love, taken hold of by the infinite beauty of the living God?

April 17

God of all loving, you welcome us at all times. Why should we wait for our hearts to be changed in order to live a life rooted in you? You offer us all we need to soothe and heal our wounds.

April 18

A believer from Bangladesh, speaking about those around him who know nothing of Christ, said, "When you are close to a fire, you are warmed. When the fire of God's love is in us, does it not shine on those who are close to us, even if we do not realize it?"

April 19

In his life on earth, Jesus needed to hear a human voice tell him, "You know that I love you." Three times he asked Peter, "Do you love me?"⁵ Christ asks each of us the very same question, age-old and always new: "Do you love me?" And he asks each of us to be attentive to those he entrusts to us.

April 20

Inner silence and peace of heart never extinguish the call to human solidarity, which comes straight from the Gospel.

April 21

Holy Spirit, mystery of a presence, you breathe in us a gentle breeze which refreshes the soul. And the unexpected occurs: once again we begin the journey from doubt towards the brightness of your face.

April 22

"Where there is love, God is present." If we can feel nothing, no need to waste time worrying about it. Where there is a living charity, God is present. Still more: he is there in fullness.

April 23

When we are assailed by feelings of inferiority, we may be surprised one day to come to this realization: the road to fulfillment lies not in prestigious gifts or great abilities, but in living charity.

April 24

Jesus our joy, the simple desire for your presence is already the beginning of faith. And as the days pass, the longing hidden within us causes springs of living water to gush forth: goodness, selflessness, and also that inner harmony that comes from the Holy Spirit in us.

April 25

When confronted with the calls of the Gospel, some people are beset by doubt and ask themselves, "Do I have enough faith?" But our faith did not create God. Nor will our doubts ever put an end to God's existence.

April 26

Forgiving is one of the most unbelievable, one of the most indispensable Gospel realities for anyone who wants to follow Christ. And a heart overflowing with kindness is close to a miracle in our lives.

April 27

By night we will go to the spring. Deep within us there sparkles living water where we can quench our thirsts.

Could the human soul be that, too: the secret heartbeat of a happiness almost beyond words?

April 28

Risen Jesus, sometimes our heart calls out to you: "I am not worthy to receive you, but only say the word and I will be healed."[6] *At the core of our life your Gospel is light within us, your Eucharist is a presence within us.*

April 29

When we seem to lose the incentive to follow Christ, we can still surrender ourselves to the Holy Spirit, entrusting everything to him.

May the day come when our heart and our spirit are once again like dry ground thirsting for him. . . . We kept on loving him, even when we had forgotten him.

April 30

Could moroseness be more contagious than peace of heart? By looking at events pessimistically, by dramatizing situations, some people attempt to acquire a certain authority. But doesn't this mean abandoning a Gospel treasure? Which one? The wonder of a love.

May

May 1

Happy are those who live in the trusting of faith; they will see God![1] How will they see him? Like Mary who, attentive, "kept everything in her heart"[2] and saw God with her inward eye.

May 2

God of all eternity, you know that our human language is almost incapable of expressing our longing for a communion with you. But you grant us the gift of a life hidden in you. And the sun rises on a new day, a day of trusting.

May 3

In the fourth century Ambrose, bishop of Milan, was deeply concerned to see that some Christians were accumulating riches. He wrote to them:

> The earth was created in common and for everyone. Nature knows no wealthy people; she only gives birth to the poor. You are not taking what is yours and giving it to the poor; you are restoring to them a portion of what belongs to them, for you have been usurping for yourself alone something given for all to use in common.

May 4

Bearers of fragility and of radiance, of the abyss and of fullness, human beings are never irrevocably doomed to the darkness of despair. Hope can be glimpsed even in a life overwhelmed by trials.

May 5

Jesus, light of our hearts, we would like to remain close to you, never abandoning you by our wayside. And when we come to know our weaknesses, unexpected resources appear within us. How could we refuse an inner vitality that comes from you?

May 6

Would you only love those who love you? Almost anybody can do that, with no need for the Gospel. But Christ calls you to love even those who hurt you and to pray for them.[3]

May 7

Attentive as we are to building up the human family, how can we remain unaware that so many peoples today reflect the mysterious figure of the "suffering servant"?[4] Humiliated, ill-treated, with nothing to attract us, they bear our diseases.

May 8

When we pray, what can we do about distractions? Not worry about them. God is familiar with our longings. He perceives better than we do our intention and what lies deep within our being. What we have trouble grasping in prayer, God has already understood.[5]

May 9

Christ Jesus, even in the obscurity of faith, even without yet seeing you clearly,[6] we believe. And you come to call us out of our slumber; you awaken us to the brightness of your light.

May 10

When faced with age-old or brand-new divisions, is it not urgent today for Christians to be reconciled by love? And when Christ calls, who can refuse? How can we forget his words?: Be reconciled without delay.[7]

Do we have hearts large enough, imaginations open enough, love burning enough to enter upon that Gospel way: to live as people who are reconciled, without delaying a single day?

May 11

You aspire to follow the Risen Christ, and you wonder by what sign you will know that you have encountered him. Are you able to understand that he is already alive in the depths of your being, in your heart of hearts? Is it still necessary to want to feel his presence?

May 12

Christ Jesus, you did not come to earth to judge the world but so that through you, the Risen Lord, every human being might be saved, reconciled.[8] And when the love that forgives burns with a Gospel flame, the heart, even when beset by trials, can begin to live again.

May 13

The Gospel assures us that the Risen Christ is always with us.[9] We can ask him, "Show us the way." And he replies, "I am here." We tell him, "You understand my prayer; it is like my childhood prayer." And the desire for a prayer that is utterly simple is always there within us.

May 14

Not resignation, but a trust that comes from the depths: surrendering ourselves to the Holy Spirit, entrusting again and yet again to the living Christ all that weighs upon our heart.

May 15

Submit to harsh events? No, consent to them instead.

And supposing it were even sometimes possible to be built up inwardly through this or that trial. . . .

May 16

Christ Jesus, you never lead us into discouragements that knock us off balance, where all we are left with is moroseness and sadness. On the contrary, you enable us to achieve a communion and even an intimacy with you. And though there may be trials in store for each person, there is above all a love which comes from you. It brings us back to life.

May 17

Should we worry if we are not thinking about God all the time? Seven hundred years ago a Christian from the Rhineland, Meister Eckhart, wrote:

> To turn to God . . . does not mean to keep thinking about God. That would be impossible . . . and in addition, it would not be the best thing. Human beings cannot be satisfied with a God that is the object of thought. For then, when the thought vanished, God would vanish too. . . . God is beyond all human thoughts. And the reality of God never disappears.

May 18

A reflection of Christ is in us. There is no point in trying to know what it consists in. So many people on earth radiate the holiness of Christ without realizing it and perhaps without even daring to believe it. And it is better that way.

May 19

God of every human being, in a world where we are bewildered by the incomprehensible suffering of the innocent, how can we be witnesses to the Gospel? Enable us to manifest, by the lives that we live, a reflection of the compassion of Christ.

May 20

Choosing Christ means walking along a single road, not several at the same time. If we wish to follow Christ and ourselves at the same time, are we not running after our own shadows?

May 21

There are elderly people full of selflessness who are absolutely essential for the younger generations. They listen, and in this way they unburden others of a load of worries. Spiritual mothers and fathers, according to the Gospel, are given to us a hundredfold.

And young people can do so much for those who no longer have their vital energies—visit them, help them to decorate or repair their homes, . . .

May 22

In the 1970s, social upheavals were so strong that at times they wounded something in the Christian consciousness. Some people have never recovered from this. So many final judgments were passed, so much harshness expressed. This pressure even caused some people to stop believing in the worth of the life they had been living up to that point. In Taizé we said: "It is not for Christians to be 'masters of worry.' They are 'servants of trust.'"

May 23

Risen Jesus, you breathe the Holy Spirit upon us.[10] *And we would like to tell you: You have the words that give life to our soul; to whom else could we go but to you, the Risen Christ?*[11]

May 24

Love is a word that is often abused. Love is easy to say. To live out a love that forgives is another thing altogether.

May 25

How many discoveries we shall make in the next world! We shall be astonished to meet people who, unacquainted with Christ, were living by him unawares.

May 26

Risen Christ, through the Gospel your voice makes itself heard softly. You tell us: "Why worry? Only one thing is necessary,[12] a heart attentive to my words and to the Holy Spirit."

May 27

When the inner self is tormented by regrets, it has difficulty in building itself up. Remaining in God in contemplative waiting opens the way to taking essential steps: consenting to our failures, to our weak points, to our own limits. Then what seemed insipid acquires a new taste. And a peace of heart comes to life.

May 28

All who place their trust in Christ encounter him.

Living for Christ means choosing a life that is sometimes exposed, and not one that is turned in on itself.

May 29

Jesus our joy, when we realize that you love us, something in us is soothed and even transformed. We ask you: What do you want of me? And by the Holy Spirit you reply: Let nothing trouble you, I am praying in you, dare to give your life.

May 30

Prayer is sometimes a simple waiting: waiting for a way forward to open up and for inner resistances to vanish. Just like us, Christ too experienced times of burning patience.

May 31

Faith asks us neither to destroy nor to exalt human desire but to gather it into an even greater desire: the thirst for God.

June

June 1

"I am living in you."[1] The Eucharist makes these words of Christ a reality even when the heart senses nothing, even for those who hardly dare hope it.

June 2

Savior of every life, in following you we choose to love and never to harden our hearts. You wish us to know a Gospel joy. And when the depths of our being are covered by a dark cloud, one way forward remains open—the way of serene trust.

June 3

In the middle of the twentieth century there appeared a man named John, born in a humble peasant family in northern Italy. When he announced the Second Vatican Council, that old man, John XXIII, pronounced words that are among the most crystal-clear imaginable. They are able to transform and even transfigure that communion of love called the Church. Here are those words of light:

> We will not try to find out who was wrong, we will not try to find out who was right, we will only say: let us be reconciled!

During the last meeting we had with him, three of us from our community were present. We understood how deeply John XXIII wished us to be at peace concerning the future of our vocation. Making circular gestures with his hands, he explained that the Church is made up of ever larger concentric circles. Rather than giving in to worries, wasn't the essential already accomplished if we went forward in peace of heart?

June 4

Are we among those who, by their trusting, open up ways of pacification around themselves? For this endeavor, the Holy Spirit's gifts will never be lacking.

June 5

Christ Jesus, multitudes of children and young people have been marked for life because they were abandoned; they are like strangers on this earth. There are some who wonder whether their life can still have any meaning.

And you assure us: "Each time you alleviate the suffering of an innocent person, you do it for me, Christ."2

June 6

There are physical forms of violence on earth, including war, torture, murder. . . . There are other more subtle forms of violence that are concealed in cunning tactics, in suspicion, mistrust, humiliation, an unkept promise. . . .

There is no violence in God. God sent Christ not to accuse us, but to call us to himself, not to condemn us, but because he loves us.3

June 7

By forgiving us, God buries our past in the heart of Christ and brings relief to the secret wounds of our being.

When we can express to God all that burdens our life and keeps us trapped beneath the weight of a judgment, then light is shed on the shadows within us. Knowing that we are listened to, understood, forgiven by God, is one of the sources of peace . . . and our heart begins to find healing.

June 8

One day when my Indian goddaughter, Marie-Sonaly, was five years old, she and I discovered a small icon of the Virgin and Child that had been hidden away. That image spoke to us beyond measure. It was the symbol of a mother's welcome. We were able to understand that her mother, like every mother who has already entered the life of eternity, continues to welcome us along with Mary, the mother of Jesus.

June 9

Jesus, love of all loving, your compassion is without limit. We are thirsting for you who tell us: "Why be afraid? Have no fear; I am here."[4]

June 10

Saying yes to God for life is fire. Centuries before the coming of Christ, the prophet Jeremiah already realized this. In discouragement he said, "I will no longer think about God; I will no longer speak in his name. . . ." But the day came when he could write, "There was a consuming fire within me, in the deepest part of my being. I wanted to repress it, but could not."[5]

June 11

Across the earth, women, men, young people, and also children are ferments of reconciliation right in the midst of the divisions that are tearing apart the human family. Filled with trust, they have everything to turn back waves of violence and hatred, everything to restore courage to those who were sunk in doubt and disenchantment, everything to support a fine human hope. Are we, or will we be, among them?

June 12

You are the God of every human being and you allow us to glimpse your mysterious presence, shining through the life of your Christ.[6] Through him we are able to know you. And you have already placed this clear certainty within us: your love is not an empty word; it is above all compassion.

June 13

When we pray and nothing seems to happen, does our prayer remain unanswered? No. The fire of a love penetrates even the arid regions, even the contradictions of our being.

In quiet trust in God, all prayer finds some kind of fulfillment. Perhaps it is different than we expected. . . . Does not God answer us with a view to a greater love?[7]

June 14

Children can be wounded by tensions in their family, by arguments between adults in their presence. They can feel rejected and this engenders an inner appeal not to be abandoned.

The question often comes to mind: What has happened in this child? Could he or she have been humiliated at school, in the street, or somewhere else? Will someone be there to help them find their way through a void that is affecting them in their heart of hearts?

Listening to a child or an adolescent requires discretion and tact so as not to make their wounds any bigger.

June 15

Christ never sets us up as judges of one another. The Gospel emphasizes the importance of inner silence, even towards those who throw us into confusion and make us suffer.

June 16

Holy Spirit, in every situation we would like to welcome you with great simplicity. And it is above all by the intelligence of the heart that you enable us to penetrate the mystery of your life within us.

June 17

When Jesus, risen from the dead, says in his Gospel, "I give you my peace,"[8] he is not offering us a life with no inner combats. He invites us to realize that our hearts find peace especially by being rooted in the spirit of mercy.

June 18

While you were lingering far from Christ Jesus, he was already waiting for you. And on his lips were these stupefying words: "In you I have placed my joy."[9]

June 19

Savior of every life, your voice makes itself heard even at the heart of our contradictions. You tell us: "Be opened!"[10] And when we are almost without words, we may discover that a single word is enough in order to pray.

June 20

In the art of music, it sometimes happens that what cannot be expressed in words draws us to prayer. A Bach concerto, for example, can allow us to perceive human entreaty with an intensity that is rarely achieved. And the veil is lifted on the hidden God of Scripture.

June 21

When human sensibilities, keenly sensitive as they can be, become wrapped in thorns, then the fire of the Holy Spirit can consume even the roots of bitterness.

June 22

Today, the century of determinism is becoming humble as some of the most qualified scientists discern an element of the unpredictable in their research. The history of humanity is not a mere succession of causes and effects. Does it not leave room for the unexpected intervention of God? And is this not true in the life of each person as well?

June 23

God our Father, we want to love you with all our strength, with all our soul.[11] *But you know that there can be resistances within us. Give us the boldness to leap over these walls, to dare to renew again and again the yes of the gift of our life.*

June 24

Before Christ's arrival on earth, John the Baptist had this intuition: The coming of Christ is not just for a few people but for all. That is one of the joyful messages of the Gospel.[12]

June 25

Happy those who root their lives in the trusting of faith! They will discover the most far-reaching mystery of all: the continual presence of the Risen Christ.

What God gives sometimes seems so great . . . and we feel so poor! He offers us what we can scarcely imagine: Christ, and the Holy Spirit, come to dwell within our hearts, irresistibly.

June 26

There are parts of the world where the faith is in decline. Where there is a void, currents of religiosity of the most variegated sort can develop. As a consequence, one question remains constantly on our mind: How can we prepare the continuities of Christ where signs of his presence are disappearing?

June 27

Bless us, Christ Jesus: you come to comfort our hearts when the incomprehensible happens—the suffering of the innocent.

June 28

In the second century Irenaeus, a Christian of the third generation, had the clear certainty of a communion in Christ. He left us these lines: "The splendor of God is a human being fully alive. The life of a human being is the contemplation of God."

June 29

And something beyond all our hopes arises. . . . How aware are we of this?: it is by giving ourselves that we forge our identity. And the day comes when we are granted what we never even expected. The roads in shadow, the long nights with almost no light, lie behind us. Dead-end situations, struggles, far from weakening us, can even help us to grow.

June 30

"Love your enemies, do good to those who hate you, pray for those who speak ill of you."[13] To understand these words of Christ, we must have made our way through inner deserts. . . .

July

July 1

Risen Jesus, give us a steadfast heart that remains faithful to the end. And if we wonder, Is this possible? your Gospel opens our eyes to the fullness of your love: it is forgiveness, it is inner light.

July 2

To go forward in trust in God, it is a good idea to cling to a few Gospel realities and to return to them constantly:

In all things peace of heart, joy, simplicity, mercy.

God has buried your past in the heart of Christ; forget in him what assails your heart.

July 3

What if doubt were to take us by surprise? That shouldn't bring us to a standstill! Even when Jesus was on earth, right beside him there were disciples experiencing doubt. To one of them he said, "Happy those who believe without having seen!"[1]

July 4

To communicate Christ, is there any light more transparent than a life steeped in forgiveness and in infinite goodness, a life in which reconciliation is lived out day after day?

July 5

God of every human being, we are longing to hear you tell us: "Arise, let your soul live!" We never wish to choose darkness or discouragement, but to welcome the radiance of praise.

July 6

If spiritual values in many countries were not being called into question, our community would not be setting in motion a whole process that consists in welcoming, week after week, young people not just from the north, east, and south of Europe, but also young Africans, Latin Americans, and Asians.

Seeing all these young faces on our hill of Taizé, we realize that they come with vital questions: What does Christ want from me? How can I find a meaning for my life in him? Without always sensing it clearly, they are trying to follow Christ. The starting-point of their search is this aspiration: How can God be everything for me?

The important thing for my brothers and myself is to respond to their trust by being above all men of prayer and of listening, never spiritual masters.

At every age, doesn't every human being need to be listened to, and to receive a "shock of meaning," as if it were the very first time?

July 7

At the same time as John XXIII, in Constantinople there was another holy witness to Christ, Patriarch Athenagoras. At the end of a visit with him, when we were saying goodbye, the patriarch stood in the doorway and, making the gesture of raising the Eucharistic chalice, said these final words: "The cup and the breaking of the bread, there is no other solution, remember!"

July 8

A believer of the first centuries wrote, "Don't be anxious!"[2] When we entrust to Christ the worries that keep us far from him, he enables us to discover this reality: "In calm and trust will be your strength."[3]

July 9

Jesus, love of all loving, you were always in me and I was forgetting you. You were in my heart of hearts and I was looking for you elsewhere. When I kept myself far from you, you were waiting for me. And now I dare to tell you: Risen Christ, you are my life.

July 10

In human beings there is a fathomless thirst for freedom. Like the most beautiful of coins, freedom can have another side. What kind of freedom would it be if, used in a self-centered way, it harmed the freedom of others? Freedom is intimately linked to forgiveness and reconciliation.

July 11

How much spiritual tact, how much attention, are necessary so that a fear of God does not enter a child's heart!

"God is love."⁴ If a life rooted in God meant fear of punishment, where would the Gospel be?

July 12

At every age, there is a need for periods of ripening. They take time. Why be impatient with oneself? Going from one beginning to another can open a way forward beyond discouragements.

July 13

Risen Christ, when we have the simple desire to welcome your love, little by little a flame is kindled in the depths of our being. Fueled by the Holy Spirit, this flame of love may be quite faint at first. The amazing thing is that it keeps on burning.

And when we realize that you love us, the trust of faith becomes our own song.

July 14

Letting the Risen Christ dwell within us and living intensely in the present moment . . . his words are so clear: "Today, I would like to enter your home."⁵ Today, not tomorrow.

July 15

To communicate faith in the Risen Christ, what would be the use of ready-made answers? May our life let the Gospel shine through!

July 16

Is prayer a matter of achieving emptiness within by silencing the imagination? When we pray, reflections and images pass through our minds. When we are surprised to find ourselves saying, "My thoughts are wandering; my heart is scattered," the Gospel replies, "God is greater than our heart."[6]

July 17

Holy Spirit, in you we find the consolation with which Christ can flood our lives. Your presence is offered to each person . . . and we sense that the essential has already been accomplished in us.

July 18

Though they are not so easy to grasp at first sight, will we let these words of Christ question us?: "Whoever gives their life for love of me will find it."[7]

How will we find it? In an existence full of attentiveness and of kindness of heart. And Christ himself will become our life.

July 19

When the night becomes dense, His love is a fire. Then what was glowing underneath the ashes bursts into flame. And even the thorns of the past feed that flame.

July 20

Nothing is more harrowing than the breakup of a deep human affection. Sometimes the heart no longer knows where it's at. To protect itself, to suffer less, it may become hardened.

When Christ was rejected, he did not rebel. And it is this Christ whom we are following.

July 21

Jesus our peace, if our lips keep silence, our heart listens to you and also speaks to you. And you say to each one of us: "Surrender yourself in all simplicity to the life of the Holy Spirit; for this, the little bit of faith you have is enough."

July 22

Dostoyevsky allows us to glimpse deep-seated doubts within him, but his love for Christ is not thereby called into question: "My 'hosanna' has passed through the crucible of doubt."

His doubt was like a purifying fire that opened the way for a reflection of Christ to penetrate deep within him.

July 23

God of all eternity, whether we know it or not, your Holy Spirit is light within us. He illuminates the shadows of our soul. He penetrates our inner nights, suffusing them with his invisible presence.

July 24

Almost all of us wish for a life free of contradictions, of conflicts. But when the foundations are shaken, is there any other way than that of a heart filled with compassion? It makes us able to pray even for those who disfigure our intentions.

July 25

The call to follow Christ places us before an alternative, the choice between all or nothing. There is no happy medium. Even when a fog of hesitations catches us unawares, we would like to listen to him when he tells us, "Come and follow me. I will lead you to the wellsprings of living water,[8] the wellsprings of the Gospel."

July 26

Jesus our peace, you never abandon us. And the Holy Spirit always opens a way forward, the way which consists in casting ourselves into God as into the depths. And astonishment arises: these depths are not an abyss of darkness; they are God, fathomless depths of compassion and innocence.

July 27

Will we be among those who, even all alone, keep on praying in a church that has been deserted by many? How often one single person has been enough so that others can take over one day.

July 28

In the course of history, one day multitudes of Christians found themselves divided without even knowing why.

Today, for the multitudes of Christians who are innocent of these divisions, is it not urgent to offer signs of great openness and to bring to life a Gospel joy, that of living as people who are reconciled each day anew?

July 29

God of every human being, you are familiar with our longing to be a reflection of your presence. And you offer us all we need to make life beautiful for those you entrust to us.

July 30

Many are those who end their lives in great isolation. Do we not sometimes discover a deep-seated loneliness among women and men advanced in age? They think they have achieved nothing. Do they have to wait until they are in the next world to understand that in them God is already everything?

July 31

Why does God not keep human beings from doing evil? He has created us free. God is love, and love never imposes itself.

August

August 1

Christ Jesus, we are searching for your face. The look in your eyes is enough to dispel sorrow and worry. And by relying on you, we can commit ourselves now and for ever to walk in your footsteps.

August 2

When we wake up each morning, if praise of the Risen Christ were to fill our hearts . . . then, in the monotony of daily life, an inner surge of vitality would reveal our hidden longing.

August 3

In this period of history, there is an unprecedented awakening of the Christian conscience with regard to suffering throughout the world. More people than ever before are concerned about human rights and a just sharing of material resources. Close to the forgotten of this earth, more and more people are looking for solutions and responses. They know that faith does not turn us into people who are irresponsible.

August 4

Jesus our joy, you want us to have hearts that are simple, a kind of springtime of the heart. And then the complications of existence do not paralyze us so much. You tell us: "Don't worry; even if you have very little faith, I, Christ, am with you always."

August 5

Why should someone who is ill or elderly worry and say, "I am not doing anything for others?" Could they have forgotten that their prayer is welcomed in God and that it will find something beyond all their hopes—a fulfillment?

August 6

A Gospel revolution in our lives: Christ enters into us by the Holy Spirit, even passing through the contradictory forces over which our will has little influence. He places a reflection of his face within us, "transfiguring" what troubles us about ourselves.

August 7

Holy Spirit, you breathe upon what is fragile. You kindle a flame of living charity and love that remains within us, still alive under the ashes. And through you, even the fears and the nights of our heart can become the dawn of a new life.

August 8

In order to leave discouragement behind and to discover a hope, don't we need most of all "living icons": witnesses to the trusting of faith?

August 9

In the Gospel, one day Jesus said to his disciples, "Let little children come to me; the Kingdom of God is for those who are like them."[1] Is not Christ utterly accessible to a simple heart?

August 10

In the course of a dialogue, when we are contradicted, even brusquely, we can find peace of heart by entrusting to the Holy Spirit those we are speaking with—and doing this, naturally, without their even realizing it.

August 11

Jesus our peace, why do we constantly keep going forward on a road towards you? Because human beings become who they really are in the presence of God. And we await your breath of life; it penetrates the depths of our being.

August 12

At this turning-point of contemporary history, some areas of the world are desert regions for faith. But at the same time, there are believers who move mountains of indifference around them when they are invigorated by a freshness of community life and are brimming over with Gospel vitality.

August 13

When the essential remains hidden from our eyes, that only makes us all the more eager to progress towards the one reality: in us God is everything.

August 14

God of all the living, by your Gospel we are made sensitive to those who experience human abandonment, violence, persecution, exile. And you call us to alleviate the sufferings of those you have entrusted to us.

August 15

It is not the powerful of the earth who determine the changes in the world. Could the Virgin Mary have thought that her life would be essential for the future of the human family? Like her, so many of the humble of the earth are preparing ways of peaceful communion.

August 16

Even while providing for material needs, a parent can be absent for all practical purposes. Alluding to the parable of the prodigal son, a young New Yorker stated, "In my family it wasn't the son who went away; it was the father who left us."

August 17

Being born and reborn through the Holy Spirit means rediscovering at every age the Gospel in its first freshness. . . . Then there is no day which cannot be God's today.

August 18

Holy Spirit, in your presence we discover that we are never alone. Still more, as we surrender ourselves to you, we understand that you give new impetus to our longing.

August 19

A spirit of festival drawn from the Gospel is not euphoria. Enthusiasm, yes, not something forced. . . . In all things serene joy.

August 20

One day almost nine centuries before Christ, in the middle of a famine, a woman from the village of Zarephath saw Elijah, the man of God, come into her house. All the food that remained was a little flour and oil. To make him welcome, the widow did not hesitate to make three cakes with what she had left. And the unexpected happened . . . the flour and the oil would not run out.[2]

Isn't this a parable for our lives? We have almost nothing stored up and yet, with this little bit, we can live that which is beyond all our hopes and which will never come to an end.

August 21

Jesus, light of our hearts, you place in us a longing accessible to our human frailty, the longing for your presence. Even without always understanding, we would like to live lives centered on the beautiful hope of the Gospel and to find there the energy to begin again.

August 22

Every human being yearns to be loved as well as to love. It is not for nothing that the Gospel alerts us about not becoming locked up in isolation.

When we are listened to, obstacles created by frustrations of the heart and wounds from a recent or distant past fall away. Being listened to is the beginning of a healing of the soul.

And the breath of a trust arises . . . and a gateway to freedom begins to open up.

August 23

For the person most devoid of knowledge, just as for the most cultivated, faith remains a humble trusting in God. If faith were to become a spiritual pretension, it would lead nowhere.

August 24

Your aspiration is to follow the Risen Christ. By what sign can you recognize that you have encountered him? When, as you come closer to him, your inner combats do not harden you but lead you to the very wellsprings of his love.

In this inner revolution, all that could have broken the fibers of the soul, feelings of uselessness, loneliness, no longer block the path. And a way forward takes shape: it always leads from worries towards trusting in God.

August 25

Savior of every human being, you open our eyes to the wonder of your compassion. It heals our hearts. And we understand your call as you say to each one of us: "Come, follow me; in me you will find rest; come."

August 26

The Holy Spirit is like a fire kindled within, an inner flame. Let his inspirations come alive, and already life becomes full!

August 27

Is the night becoming dark? Let us look towards the light of the Risen Christ "until day breaks and the morning star rises in our hearts."[3] And an imperceptible inner transformation, a transfiguration of our being, continues our whole life long.

August 28

Christ dwells in us! Do we not need time to prepare ourselves inwardly to grasp this Gospel reality, almost inaccessible to the human intelligence?

Four centuries after Christ an African Christian named Augustine wrote, "Christ is within you; his dwelling is there. Present your prayer to him but do not shout as if he were far away. He is in your very depths."[4]

August 29

Holy Spirit, Spirit of the Risen Christ, by turning us towards you in the present moment, you make it possible for us to cross the deserts of the heart. By your forgiveness, "you dissipate our faults like the morning mist."[5] There we find Christian freedom; there lies the wonder of a love.

August 30

How could my brothers and I live in the West if part of our community were not present in the midst of the poorest in the southern continents?

When we remember that some of our brothers are sharing in living conditions of great poverty, we know that such a gift of the self is a burning breath of the Gospel. Even from afar it penetrates our vocation.

August 31

For whoever knows how to love, for whoever knows how to suffer with Christ, life is filled with serene beauty.

Some days may bring disappointments, bitter tastes—accidents that can cause peace of heart to vanish. But every day there remains the longing for his coming. A day is complete when the most difficult consequences of a trial do not manage to halt the momentum towards fulfillment.

September

September 1

Nothing is more enduring than the memory of past humiliations and wounds. Such memories foster an attitude of suspiciousness, sometimes lasting several generations. Gospel forgiveness, on the other hand, enables us to go beyond the memory.

Will we be among those who gather up their energies to curb all forms of mistrust, be they age-old or brand-new?

September 2

God of all the living, enable us to surrender ourselves to you in silence and in love. Surrendering ourselves to you does not come easily to our human condition. But you intervene in the deepest recesses of our being and your will for us is the radiance of a hope.

September 3

If prayer itself were to become secularized in order to be made more relevant, then perhaps humble symbols that communicate the invisible presence would be eliminated. And as a result, would not certain regions deep within our being no longer be touched as much?

September 4

If the beginning of a yes for life sometimes includes an element of human error, will that not be burnt away by the fire of the Holy Spirit? And this fire will illuminate the Gospel call: "There is no greater love than to give one's life."[1]

September 5

When someone we have loved dearly dies, someone who in addition was a support for us, the trial can go so far as to undermine our hope. Rediscovering the trusting of faith and peace of heart sometimes requires having a great deal of patience with ourselves.

Have we become so frail that the depths of our being need to be comforted? Christ sends the Holy Spirit, the Comforter. And the pain of a great separation can be transfigured into a communion that is at one and the same time so mysterious and so indispensable.

September 6

Jesus, joy of our hearts, when the impression that we cannot fulfill what you expect of us comes welling up inside us, haven't you responded already? You invite us to love, just as you love us.[2]

September 7

Attempting to live for Christ in the midst of others, who will dare to go to the utmost of their strength in order to forgive and forgive again? That is the extreme of loving.

September 8

In humble trust in God, the Virgin Mary did not keep her Son for herself; she offered him to the world. Don't we, in our turn, wish to give what God gives us?

September 9

Prayer opens us up to a boundless communion. With no beginning nor end, the realities of God, of Christ, of the Holy Spirit, cannot be measured. Often it is only afterwards that we grasp the continual presence of Christ, the Risen Lord: "So! He was there the whole time; it was him!"

September 10

Holy Spirit, inner light, you shine in the happy days as well as in the times in our life when we undergo trials. And when the daylight seems to disappear, your presence remains. It forges our inner self. It enables us to go forward from one beginning to another.

September 11

When a springtime of the Church is a long time coming, the Holy Spirit already allows it to blossom in those who are waiting for it. Could God refuse to let our deserts flower?

September 12

Doesn't a contemplative outlook, focused on God, rescue us from the grayness of routine, from monotony? Permeated by the Gospel, such an outlook is also capable of perceiving the treasures of a heart warmed by infinite goodness.

September 13

There were periods in history when some Christians were particularly sensitive to sharing. In the fourth century Saint John Chrysostom wrote, "Quarrels and wars break out because some people try to take for themselves what belongs to everyone. It is as if nature became indignant that human beings, by means of those cold words *yours* and *mine,* have sowed division where God has set unity. The words *yours* and *mine* are meaningless."

September 14

Living God, if some difficulty in believing happens to come our way, why should we worry? Being in your presence in a peaceful silence is already praying. And you understand all that we are. Even our sighs become a quite humble prayer.

September 15

Who will find ways to open up children and young people to trust in Christ? Take a child by the hand, go with that child into a church to pray in silence . . . and he or she will be awakened to the mystery of God. An intuition of faith, no matter how feeble, even if it has been forgotten, often reappears later on in life.

A space remains empty inside us when there has been no awakening to faith in childhood. It gets filled in whatever way possible, sometimes using elements of religiosity that are utterly foreign to God and to Christ.

September 16

Sometimes we wish for signs or portents that are immediately visible. But why look far away for what is so close at hand? Do we not discern a light flickering in the Gospel? And already that light rises in our hearts.[3]

September 17

When the weight of a discouragement overwhelms you to the point of abandoning Christ, will you put off coming back to the inner oasis in your heart of hearts, that intimate place where God is everything? And when you remember Christ's call once again, will you make your life a response to it, a response of wonder?

September 18

Christ of compassion, we dare to tell you everything. Enable us to speak to you like the child we used to be.

September 19

One day, Christ blessed five loaves of bread and distributed them to everyone without distinction.[4] Long ago this story inspired Christians to discover a sign of hospitality: giving blessed bread to all those, both believers and nonbelievers, who for different reasons do not receive the Eucharist.

Doesn't this humble gesture lead us to ponder on the Church's motherly love, manifested when it inspires signs of wide openness, signs that reflect a mystery of communion?

September 20

Our whole life long, far from letting us slip into the abyss of discouragement, Christ offers new vitality over and over again. . . . A little springtime is here. Each of us has to open our window to it!

September 21

There are vast numbers of people who have come close to the holiness of Christ by the gift of their lives. They heard the words Jesus speaks to each person: "Come, follow me!" Who could reply to this call by saying, "I have something else to do right now; I will follow you later"?[5]

September 22

God of all eternity, open in us the gates of a communion with you; open, for it is coming, the breath of your Word. And we understand that the will of your love is not a harsh law, written on tablets of stone. It consists in living charity, written on our hearts.[6]

September 23

We are often asked why so many young people come to Taizé. What answer can we give? We were not prepared for it. The years pass and we are no less astonished.

From the beginnings of Taizé, we realized that it was essential to live in a mutual trust with the younger generations. We wanted to see a capacity for trust develop in the young; it is a lever to provide a way out of the crisis of confidence in humanity that has marked the end of the twentieth century.

Sometimes we ask ourselves whether the welcome we offer here is not too rudimentary, too poor. And we discover that with great simplicity of heart and with very few resources we are enabled to accomplish a Gospel hospitality that did not seem possible.

September 24

The basis of our life is to welcome the love of God, of Christ, of the Holy Spirit. Doesn't everything spring from such trust?

September 25

In each person there dwells an element of the unknown, and even doubts that come from who knows where. But in the depths of our being, the Holy Spirit prays more than we realize. And one day the chasms within will be filled by a prayer steeped in silence.

September 26

*Christ Jesus, you were a human being; you know how humans
aspire to inner peace. Our soul asks you: "Give us peace within."
And in our darkness, you kindle the fire of your forgiveness and
your compassion, a fire which never dies away.*

September 27

Today, isn't that communion of love which is the Body of Christ,
his Church, entering a period when it is being stripped to the
essentials? Perhaps its credibility is at stake. This is all the more
so since, in some parts of the world, people are moving away from
the faith.

September 28

A Christian who lived sixteen hundred years ago, Saint
Augustine, left behind some words that open wide the gates of
the Gospel. He struggled a great deal in order to come to God. He
suffered from his behavior as a young man. He was so honest
with himself that at times he must have despaired of his own
self. Then one day he was able to write down these words: "If you
desire to see God, you already have faith."

September 29

In whoever lives the first of the Beatitudes, "Happy the simple in heart,"[7] Christ allows the light of the Gospel to shine, incomparably. And simplicity brings to birth, all unexpected, a peaceful joy.

September 30

Jesus, peace of our hearts, in the Gospel you ask the question: "Who am I for you?"[8] You are the one who searches tirelessly for us. In your life on earth, you were affected to the depths of your being; you wept at the death of someone you loved.[9] And for you, Christ, loving is expressed in an infinite goodness of heart.

October

October 1

Humble prayer is within the reach of everyone. Sharing with Christ in all simplicity enables us to be with him one day. The apostle Paul knew this when he wrote, "We do not know how to pray, but the Holy Spirit comes to help us in our inability and prays within us."[1]

October 2

An equal trust shown to all the peoples of the earth, and not just to some, opens a way to peace. In every nation, there is a small number of demented persons who are capable, if they come to power, of drawing the masses into the vortex of hatred and war. For this reason it is crucial never to humiliate members of a nation when a few of its leaders have triggered unbelievable violence.

Are we sufficiently aware that no one people is more guilty than others—such a thing doesn't exist and never will.

October 3

Jesus our peace, where the trusting of faith has been shaken you make us bearers of your Gospel, and you keep us close to those who are paralyzed by doubt.

October 4

There are countless Christians who undergo an inner struggle, and sometimes suffering, in order to be bearers of peace in that communion of love which is the Church. They are not naive when confronted with abuses that undermine communion. They could criticize the inflexible attitudes of some people. Far from allowing themselves to be drawn in that direction, they strive for silence and love with all their soul. When they express their desires, they are careful not to dig ditches that could separate people still more. They search for all that stimulates us to live as people who are already reconciled.

October 5

Trust in Christ is not conveyed by means of arguments which attempt to persuade at all costs and thus end up causing anxiety, and even fear.

October 6

Happy those who can say: I live for God! Happy those who draw the meaning of their life from the crystal-clear fountain of God!

October 7

God of all the living, we are longing for the breath of your Holy Spirit. He causes a spring of living water to well up, a Gospel joy.

October 8

In the presence of physical violence or moral torture a question plagues us: If God is love, where does evil come from?

No one can explain the why of evil. In the Gospel, Christ enters into solidarity with the incomprehensible suffering of the innocent. Did he not come to earth so that every human being might know that he or she is loved?

October 9

There are young people who were abandoned as children. A void has opened up in them and they want to fill it. When their depths cry out in loneliness, the ultimate question rises from deep within them: Does my life have any meaning? For some, it is as if they wanted to run and keep on running to find a father, a mother. . . . Who will understand them?

October 10

Christ Jesus, we want to go to your wellspring, in days of joy as well as in days of worry. And you will speak to us by the Holy Spirit and we shall listen to your voice, filled with your love and with living charity.

October 11

In the most somber moments, when Christians experience intense discouragement, what else can we do except to cast ourselves into that fathomless depth which is the hope that springs from faith?

October 12

Before the universe began, from all eternity, Christ was in God. Since the birth of humanity, he has been a living Word.[2] Then he dwelt among us on earth as a poor man. Risen from the dead, by the Holy Spirit he remains alongside each person.

October 13

We do not forgive out of self-interest, in order to change the other person, for example. That would be a stratagem which has nothing to do with the selfless love found in the Gospel. We forgive on account of Christ.

Forgiving means not even seeking to know what the other person will do with that forgiveness.

October 14

Jesus our joy, because your forgiveness radiates trust, peace of heart is possible and even certain. Your Gospel tells us: "Why be upset? You can change nothing by worrying about it."[3]

October 15

The essence of prayer never changes, yet it can take on a host of different expressions.

There are people who pray in a great silence. Others need many words. Saint Theresa of Avila wrote, "When I speak to the Lord, often I do not know what I am saying." Others find heaven's joy on earth, a fulfillment, in prayer together with other people.

October 16

Are we going to listen to the call that comes to us right from the time of the Gospel?: "Do not put out the Spirit's flame."[4] Upheld as we are by the breath of the Holy Spirit, will we realize that he is at work within us, stimulating us, bringing us out of darkness and leading us towards the light? He reorients the depths of our being. And in our heart of hearts we discover that a portion of ourselves remains solid and unshakable.

October 17

Holy Spirit, you lift the veil that would otherwise cover our eyes and we see that God's mercy is boundless. And our resistance to living lives of forgiveness melts away.

October 18

Luke's Gospel ends with the image of the disciples bowing low with their foreheads to the ground.[5] In this way they take up a prayer posture that perhaps goes back to the remotest origins of humanity. It expresses the silent offering of one's life.

October 19

Does it not sometimes happen that, without realizing it, the older generations prepare a way forward for the young towards trust in God? Young people from one of the Baltic countries said:

> If we have become believers and if we are here in Taizé, it is because of our grandmothers. Most of them were sent away from their country for many years. Over there, in the place to which they were deported, all they had to keep them going was faith. They are simple women. They did not understand the reason for so much suffering. Some have come back; they are transparent and without bitterness. For us now, our grandmothers are saints.

October 20

In the communion of the Church, choosing Christ can lead to essential forms of detachment, for example by giving up power over others.

October 21

God our Father, you never stop searching for all who have gone away from you. And by your forgiveness, you place on our finger the ring of the prodigal son, the ring of festival.[6]

October 22

Could you have forgotten the presence of the Risen Christ? There is nothing surprising about that. Surrender yourself to him, say a few words to him, express an intention . . . and you will find him wherever you happen to be, in the street, at work, at home.

October 23

When things to be done and meetings proliferate, if emergencies come bursting in on our daily activity, doesn't the Risen Christ offer the most astonishing support? At every age, within us there is such an inner call to rely on him.

October 24

Through the face of a human being, especially when tears and sufferings have made it more transparent, it becomes possible to glimpse a reflection of the face of Christ himself.

October 25

Breath of God's loving, Holy Spirit, if we pray, if we place our trust in you, it is because you lead us to discover this surprising reality: God creates neither fear nor anguish in us; all God can do is love us.

October 26

Prayer is a serene force at work in human beings. It keeps them from growing unfeeling in the face of the turmoils experienced by whole sectors of humankind. From it are drawn vital energies of compassion.

October 27

In the course of our Christian life we are enabled to pass from one beginning to another beginning. But this process burns out if it does not draw its energy from an underground and almost intangible communion, the invisible presence of the Holy Spirit.

October 28

If solitary prayer can be arduous, the beauty of prayer with others is an incomparable support to the inner life. Through simple words, hymns, songs, it communicates a discreet and silent joy.

October 29

Jesus, love of all loving, in the plowed-up earth of our lives you come to place the trusting of faith. A small seed at first, faith can become within us one of the most unmistakable Gospel realities. It sustains the inexhaustible goodness of a human heart.

October 30

God understands all our human languages. He understands our words, and our silences too. Silence is sometimes all there is to prayer.

October 31

The vast possibilities of science and technology are able to alleviate sufferings, and to put an end to famines, in the human family as it grows to unprecedented proportions.

Indispensable though they may be, these powerful means by themselves are not enough. If we were to wake up, one fine morning, in societies that were functional, highly technological, but where the confidence of faith, the intelligence of the heart, and a thirst for reconciliation had been extinguished, what then would be the future of the human family?

November

November 1

Living God, we praise you for the multitudes of women, men, young people, and children who, across the earth, are striving to be witnesses to peace, trust, and reconciliation.

In the steps of the holy witnesses of all the ages, from the apostles and the Virgin Mary down to those of today, enable us day after day to dispose ourselves inwardly to place our trust in the Mystery of the Faith.

November 2

Trust in the resurrection enables us to realize that a communion between believers is not interrupted by death.

In simplicity of heart, we can ask those we love and who have gone before us into eternity's life, "Pray for me; pray with me." During their life on earth, their prayer supported us. After their death, how could we stop relying on them?

November 3

Who could choose the vocation to a life in community in order to attain their own individual well-being? No, that's not the road!

To be happy in community? Yes. And when all are following Christ together, all without exception, community life becomes a kind of message of joy, even in the most somber hours.

November 4

Holy Spirit, Spirit of consolation, our heart of hearts is longing to be permeated by a peaceful faith. Illuminated by your light, we glimpse the mystery of our life, and the nights of the soul are dispelled.

November 5

Baptized in the Holy Spirit, we have been clothed in Christ for ever. And God can say to each one of us, "You are the only one for me; in you I find my joy."[1]

In the tenth century a Christian named Saint Symeon wrote, "Christ will come to each person as if he were concerned with that person alone." *Thus,*

November 6

When some people experience an inner void, they wonder, But where is God?[2] And yet does not Christ, risen from the dead, remain alongside each person, even those who are unaware of him? Is not every human being visited by the Spirit of God?

November 7

Christ Jesus, enable us not to forget one thing: If faith, hope, and love are the basis of our existence, it is living love that matters above all.[3] And you tell us, "I, Christ, love you. That is the source of peace of heart."

November 8

Everywhere across the earth, perhaps more than ever before, Christians are concerned about taking on responsibilities, often very specific ones, to make the earth a better place to live in. And how astonishing it is to discover all that is made possible by a love drawn from the wellsprings of faith!

November 9

Could you be going through one of those periods when everything seems to be all dried up? At such times when nothing seems to be happening, with almost nothing a desert flower can blossom.

November 10

Savior of every life, let those who are seeking you rejoice. In one of the pages of the Gospel you tell us: "I'm familiar with your trials and your poverty, and yet you are filled."[4] *Filled by what? By the living springs hidden in the depths of your being.*

November 11

Christ knows what an inner combat we can sometimes wage in order to be found transparent. This struggle within is a sign of our love for him.

But our life is not one of constant struggle. Faith is a gift from God, never a constraint. As we welcome the Gospel's message of joy, the Holy Spirit brings us what we often did not expect—peace of heart and also a happiness.

November 12

Praised be the Risen Christ for loving us always, even when we feel nothing—or almost nothing—of his continual presence.

November 13

Risen Jesus, mystery of a presence, you never want us to be tormented; you clothe us in your peace. And when God's joy comes, it is capable of touching the depths of the soul.

November 14

Among the children who come each day to the prayer services in Taizé, one day there was a brother and a sister. The little girl, totally absorbed, kept her hands folded; her lips whispered a few words. The little boy, his hands over his eyes, remained silent. With or without words, their faces and gestures expressed the beauty of an inner life.

November 15

Hoping against all hope,[5] advancing towards the wellsprings of faith, believers change the course of certain evolutions of human history even without being very numerous.

November 16

There is no technique for praying; there is no method to achieve inner silence. If our prayer is only stammering, that hardly matters. Are we not, all of us, Christ's poor?

November 17

Living God, however poor our prayer is, we search for you with confidence. And your love carves out a way forward through our hesitations and even through our doubts.

November 18

The Gospel speaks of a young man who was seeking the will of God's love. He came to Christ with his questions. Jesus replied to him, "You are lacking one thing: sell what you have, give it to the poor, then come, follow me." And the young man went away sad.[6] Why did he go away? He did not have the inner freedom to give himself.

November 19

"Jesus, light of my heart, do not let my darkness speak to me." In writing that prayer, Saint Augustine had this intuition: When our inner darkness invites us to a conversation with itself, a dialogue takes place not with the Risen Christ but with what hurts us both in ourselves and in others. Where can that lead? Nowhere at all.

November 20

God our Father, enable us always to remember that you love us. And when we understand that nothing can separate us from you, the trust of faith opens for us the road that leads upward towards a peace-filled joy.

November 21

Icons can enhance the beauty of a prayer. They are like windows open on the realities of God.

There are artists' hands that give us a glimpse of Gospel reflections; they know how to make the mystery of God accessible to our eyes.

November 22

The apostle Peter saw Jesus during his life on earth. But with the deep realism of his faith he well knew that "We love Christ without having seen him and, though we still do not see him, we place our trust in him." And he could go on to write, "We are filled with a joy beyond words that already transfigures us."[7]

November 23

Will we be among those who spread the fine hope of a new future? To prepare this, who will open up ways of conciliation where hatred and violence are exploding? Who will uphold freedoms in places where they are still quite young?

November 24

Christ of compassion, you enable us to turn to you . . . and inner light rises in our hearts.[8] *Then we can pray with these words: Jesus, my joy, my hope, and my life.*

November 25

Happy those who draw from the Risen Christ a trust that will never die away, that will never wear out!

November 26

Christ does not turn us into people who have made it. He keeps us close to him, as transparent as the sky in springtime, a springtime that awakens.

November 27

Jesus, joy of our hearts, your Gospel assures us that the Kingdom of God is in our midst,[9] *and the gates of simplicity, and those of innocence, open within us.*

November 28

One day, Jesus spoke grave words regarding "those who lay heavy burdens on other people's shoulders, but are unwilling to lift a finger themselves to move them."[10]

November 29

To respond to Christ's call to the very end, prepare yourself for fidelities. In you will be forged a humanity permeated with kindness—not an illusory love that would be satisfied with words, but a heart as wide as the world.

November 30

Some parents are concerned when they see their children leaving the places where they themselves pray. But will not the best of their faith appear again when the children grow up and have to take on important responsibilities? The fine flower of trust in God, glimpsed in childhood, is not lost for ever. Its scent invisibly pervades the soul.

December

December 1

Whoever responds to the Gospel's calls refuses to consider anyone an enemy.[1] Praying in silence and love, they find enough freedom even to forgive those who are distorting their intentions.

December 2

Holy Spirit, mystery of a presence, you penetrate the depths of our being and there you discern our longing. You know what our intention is—to communicate your love and your compassion through an infinite goodness of heart.

December 3

However little we understand of the Gospel, it is light in our midst. However little we perceive of the Holy Spirit, he is life for us. However little we grasp of the Eucharist, it is Christ's presence in us.

December 4

Our heart finds peace in knowing that death is not the end. Death opens the way towards a life where God welcomes us to himself for ever.

When she was already very elderly, my mother had a heart attack. As soon as she could speak again she uttered these words: "I am not afraid of dying; I know who I believe in . . . but I love life." And on the day she died she whispered, "Life is beautiful. . . ."

December 5

In prayer, God does not ask us to accomplish wonders that are too much for us. But God does enable us to surrender ourselves to him in great simplicity. And the Holy Spirit suggests simple words: "Christ, what do you want from me?"

December 6

In the troubles of human life, a way forward from darkness to the light of Christ constantly opens up. It is as if Christ came to illuminate the section of road along which we are walking, as if his light followed our steps to illuminate one of the Gospel secrets within us.

What is this secret? It is disposing ourselves to place our trust in Christ, today, tomorrow, and throughout our life.

December 7

God of all loving, you call us to live lives rooted in you. Even were we to leave you, by your Holy Spirit you remain present. And your presence in us is not for one moment only, but for all time.

December 8

The Virgin Mary sheds light on the mystery of offering. A Puerto Rican woman understood this when she wrote the following words to her son as he was committing himself by a yes for his entire lifetime:

> When I discovered your total love for God, I thought of the Virgin Mary. As a mother, she consented to what God had prepared. My son, what can I do when God is acting? I cannot refuse to give God what belongs to him. You are all that I have but, because of the love God has for us, we give him everything.

December 9

The astonishing presence of the Holy Spirit is a fire. Even when it is a pale glimmer, suddenly it flares up within. It keeps on burning even when we have the impression that we do not know how to pray.

December 10

In the Gospel there are words that are unique. Is it not a miracle that they have come all the way down to us? One example of this are the words of the apostle Paul when he writes, "You are already risen with Christ."[2]

Though we all die in our bodies, for each of us the resurrection has already begun here on earth. At times when this conviction becomes hard to grasp, we can say to God, "Do not look at what little faith I have, but enable me to rely on the faith of your whole Church, on the faith of so many humble witnesses who have rooted their lives in you to a point beyond compare."

December 11

Risen Christ, by the Holy Spirit who always dwells in our hearts, you go down into the arid regions of our being. And you open a way ahead on which nothing is disastrous except losing the spirit of mercy.

December 12

Many people today have to live in the midst of noise. A few moments of silence during the day are all the more indispensable.

When we join others for prayer, a time of silence likewise has an incalculable worth.

Does not silence in a personal relationship with God build us up within? Remaining in the presence of the Holy Spirit through long periods of inner silence, even if nothing seems to be happening there and then, allows us to mature both the decisions of each day and the great decisions of an entire lifetime.

December 13

Prayer does not require superhuman efforts. Like a soft sigh, like a child's prayer, it keeps us alert. Has not God revealed to Christ's poor what the powerful of this world do not understand straightaway?[3]

December 14

The more we share with simplicity what we have, the more life becomes welcoming for those entrusted to us. Simplifying enables us to offer a welcome to others, even with very little.

December 15

Holy Spirit, in a simple prayer, you enable us to reach Christ's own heart, drawing near to his holiness. Close to him, we hear his call to live each day as God's today.

December 16

Why do we force our lips to express a prayer when for the time being they refuse to do so? The mind and heart manage quite well without the use of words. And God understands.

December 17

If those who are called to speak about the Gospel or to pray aloud in front of others could say to themselves: "May your prayer and your words never contain a threat in the name of God!" God is love. He does not make use of fear to impose himself upon human beings. Even when Christ was mistreated, he did not threaten anyone.[4]

December 18

Holy Spirit, Spirit of consolation, there are times when we are beset by inner loneliness. Then you offer us enough trust to sense that Christ wants to bring relief to our hearts; he strives to be everything for us.

December 19

To consent: there are people for whom this is their motto from youth. To consent to almost inexplicable situations where it seems that only one road remains open—placing our worries in Christ. And God maintains us in an innocence which refreshes the soul.

December 20

Who is this Christ we are following?

He is the one who gives us this essential reality: to live in a communion with him. Risen from the dead, he remains alongside us—today, tomorrow, and always. In him the wellsprings of jubilation never run dry.[5]

December 21

Some people are troubled by the impression that God is silent, as if his presence were linked to what we feel. But God is still present even when any apparent resonance fades away.

December 22

God of all loving, often we forget that we bear within us the burning presence of the Holy Spirit. But you are familiar with our human condition; you know how forgetful we are, even of what is most essential. And you enable us to remain simply in your presence, waiting in all humility.

December 23

In the depths of our being has been set a call to inner freedom. And in this freedom there is poetry. It can find joy in a trifle—the wind in the trees, the play of light in the sky, the intimacy of a simple meal, the presence of those we love, of children, . . .

December 24

If each night in our lives could become a kind of Christmas night, a night illuminated from within . . .

December 25

Jesus, son of the Virgin Mary, at Christmas you offer us the joyful message of your Gospel. All who listen, all who welcome the gifts of the Holy Spirit, by day as well as in the vigils of the night, discover that with very little faith, with almost nothing, they have everything.

December 26

Not knowing how to make himself understood, God came to earth himself, poor and humble. If Christ Jesus had not lived among us, God would remain far-off, inaccessible. Jesus allows us to see God shining through his life as a human being.[6]

December 27

Were it possible to fathom a human heart, the surprising thing would be to discover there the silent longing for a presence. In John's Gospel, there appears a response to this longing: "Someone you do not know is among you."[7] Is he not always in our midst, this Christ with whom we may be almost unacquainted?

December 28

How aware are we that, for God, a human being is "sacred by the wounded innocence of his childhood"?

December 29

Jesus our joy, you tell us in your Gospel: "Look at the birds of the sky and the lilies of the field, are you not worth more than they? Why be anxious?"[8]

December 30

As we go from one beginning to another, if we could prepare ourselves to welcome every new day as if it were unique . . .

And the Risen Christ says to each person, "I will never leave you."⁹

December 31

On days when we look back, filled with regrets, our energies are depleted.

In all things peace of heart, serene joy. The Holy Spirit has buried our past in the heart of Christ. And he will take care of our future.

Some passages from the Bible dealing with trust and peace of heart

In the midst of his suffering, Job said: "I know that my Redeemer is alive, and that at the end he will rise up upon the earth. After I awake, he will set me beside him." (Job 19: 25–26)

In God alone my soul finds rest;
from him comes salvation.
In God alone my soul finds rest;
my hope comes from him.
Trust in him at all times, my people;
pour out your heart before him.
God is our refuge!
(Psalm 62:1, 5, 8)

The Lord is kind and just;
our God is merciful.
The Lord watches over the simple:
I was weak, and he saved me.
Return, my soul, to your rest.
(Psalm 116:5–7)

Lord, my heart is not proud;
I do not set my sights too high.
I do not run after great things,
things beyond my comprehension.
No, I have kept my soul still and quiet
like a child in its mother's arms;
like a little child, so is my soul within me.
(Psalm 131:1–2)

The Lord says: "Your salvation is in returning and rest; your strength lies in quiet and in confident trust." (Isaiah 30:15)

"I know the plans I have for you," says the Lord. "Plans for peace and not for misfortune, to give you a future and hope." (Jeremiah 29:11)

The Lord says: "I will give you a new heart; I will place within you a new spirit. I will take from your bodies the heart of stone and give you a heart of flesh. I will place my spirit within you." (Ezekiel 36:26–27)

Jesus said: "Come to me all you who are weary and overburdened, and I will give you rest." (Matthew 11:28)

As the storm was shaking their boat, Jesus said to his disciples: "Courage! It is I; don't be afraid!" (Matthew 14:27)

Jesus said to his disciples: "Which of you can add a single hour to his life by worrying about it? If you cannot even do such a simple thing, what point is there in worrying about all the rest?" (Luke 12:25–26)

Jesus said to his disciples: "I have told you these things while I am still with you. But the Advocate, the Holy Spirit whom the

Father will send in my name, will teach you everything and will remind you of all I said to you. I leave you peace; my peace is the gift I give you. . . . Do not let your hearts be troubled or afraid." (John 14:25–27)

Jesus said to his disciples: "I have told you these things so that in me you may have peace." (John 16:33)

Saint Paul wrote: "God's Reign is justice, peace, and joy in the Holy Spirit." (Romans 14:17)

Saint Paul wrote: "May God the Father strengthen your inner self through his Spirit. May he make Christ dwell in your hearts through faith so that, rooted and grounded in love, you may receive the ability to grasp, together with all God's holy people, what is the width, the length, the height, and the depth . . . and to know the love of Christ, which is beyond all knowledge, so that you may be filled to overflowing with all the fullness of God." (Ephesians 3:16–19)

Saint Paul wrote: "With all humility, gentleness, and patience, accept one another in love, eager to remain one in the Spirit, linked together by the bond of peace." (Ephesians 4:2–3)

Saint Paul wrote: "Once you were darkness; now you are light in the Lord. Conduct yourselves as people who belong to the light." (Ephesians 5:8)

Saint Paul wrote: "If there is any encouragement in belonging to Christ, any comfort in love, any communion in the Spirit, any affection and compassion, then make my joy complete by striving for the same goal, sharing the same love, being one in heart and soul." (Philippians 2:1–2)

Saint Paul wrote: "Rejoice in the Lord always! I will say it again: Rejoice! Let everyone see how serene you are. The Lord is near. Do not worry about anything, but in all things, by means of prayers and petitions offered with thanksgiving, make known your requests to God. And the peace of God, which is beyond all understanding, will keep your hearts and minds rooted in Christ Jesus." (Philippians 4:4–7)

Saint Paul wrote: "As people chosen by God, holy and dearly loved, clothe yourselves in feelings of compassion, kindness, humility, gentleness, and patience. Put up with one another and forgive each other if anyone has a cause for complaint against anyone else; just as the Lord forgave you, you do the same. And over everything else put on love: that is the bond that unites them all perfectly. Let Christ's peace reign in your hearts; in it you have been called to form one body. And be grateful." (Colossians 3:12–15)

Saint Paul wrote: "Avoid irreverent and empty discussions, which only lead further and further away from God." (2 Timothy 2:16)

James, the disciple of Jesus, wrote: "No one who is being tempted should say 'This temptation comes from God.' God cannot be tempted to do evil, and he never tempts anyone." (James 1:13)

Peter, the disciple of Jesus, wrote: "You love Christ although you have not seen him, and although you still do not see him, you believe, and are filled to overflowing with a joy too deep for words and radiant with God's glory." (1 Peter 1:8b)

Saint Peter wrote: "When insulted, Christ did not insult in return. When he suffered he did not threaten, but placed his trust in God." (1 Peter 2:23)

Saint Peter wrote: "Entrust all your worries to God, since he takes care of you." (1 Peter 5:7)

John, the disciple of Jesus, wrote: "My little children, we must not love just in words or with our lips, but truly, by our actions. This is how we shall know that we belong to the truth, and in God's presence our hearts will be at peace even if our hearts condemn us, because God is greater than our hearts, and he knows everything. (1 John 3:18–20)

Saint John wrote: "God is love, and whoever remains in love remains in God and God in him. . . . When we love we have no fear, since perfect love casts out fear, and anyone who is still afraid of punishment has not reached the perfection of love." (1 John 4:16b, 18)

Notes

JANUARY

1. Matthew 11:28–29
2. 1 John 4:8, 16
3. See John 3:17
4. Matthew 25:40
5. John 1:5
6. Psalm 62:1–2
7. John 14:27
8. See 1 Kings 19:9–13
9. *Gaudium et Spes* 22:2
10. See Matthew 3:11
11. See 1 Thessalonians 5:19
12. Psalm 42:7
13. Matthew 16:25

FEBRUARY

1. See Luke 2:22–24
2. John XXIII, *Journal of a Soul*
3. Luke 9:62
4. See 1 Peter 1:8
5. Matthew 11:28–29
6. *Letter to Diognetus*

MARCH

1. See John 1:1–3
2. Luke 23:34
3. See 2 Corinthians 4:7
4. See Mark 4:27
5. Proverbs 30:16
6. Psalm 84:6
7. Jeremiah 2:13
8. Luke 1:38
9. See 1 Peter 5:7
10. Revelation 3:20;
    Mark 10:21

HOLY WEEK and PENTECOST

1. See Matthew 26:38, 40–41
2. See 1 Peter 2:23
3. See Matthew 16:24
4. See Matthew 11:28
5. See 1 Peter 3:18–20; 4:6
6. See John 14:16, 26; 16:7

APRIL
1. Mark 9:24
2. See Luke 24:13–35
3. 1 John 3:20
4. See John 21:15–17
5. John 21:15–17
6. See Matthew 8:8

MAY
1. See Matthew 5:8
2. Luke 2:19, 51
3. Matthew 5:44
4. See Isaiah 53:2–4, 7
5. See Romans 8:26–27
6. See 1 Peter 1:8
7. See Matthew 5:23–24
8. See John 3:17
9. See Matthew 28:20
10. See John 20:22
11. John 6:68
12. See Luke 10:42

JUNE
1. See John 6:56; 14:20; 15:4–5
2. See Matthew 25:40
3. *Letter to Diognetus*
4. Mark 4:40; 6:50
5. Jeremiah 20:9
6. See John 14:9
7. See 1 John 5:14–15
8. John 14:27; 20:19–21
9. See Mark 1:11
10. Mark 7:34

11. See Luke 10:27
12. See Luke 3:6, 18
13. See Luke 6:27–28

JULY
1. John 20:29
2. Philippians 4:6
3. See Isaiah 30:15
4. 1 John 4:8, 16
5. Luke 19:5
6. 1 John 3:20
7. Luke 9:24
8. Isaiah 49:10

AUGUST
1. Matthew 19:14
2. See 1 Kings 17:7–16
3. 2 Peter 1:19
4. Saint Augustine, *Confessions*
5. See Isaiah 44:22

SEPTEMBER
1. John 15:13
2. See John 15:12
3. See 2 Peter 1:19
4. See Matthew 14:13–21
5. See Luke 9:59–62
6. See Jeremiah 31:33; 2 Corinthians 3:3
7. Matthew 5:3

8. Matthew 16:15
9. See John 11:35

OCTOBER

1. Romans 8:26
2. See John 1:1–10
3. See Matthew 6:27
4. 1 Thessalonians 5:19
5. See Luke 24:52
6. See Luke 15:22

NOVEMBER

1. Mark 1:11
2. See Psalm 42:3
3. See 1 Corinthians 13:13
4. Revelation 2:9
5. Romans 4:18
6. See Mark 10:17–22
7. 1 Peter 1:8
8. See 2 Peter 1:19
9. See Luke 17:21
10. Matthew 23:4

DECEMBER

1. See Matthew 5:44
2. Colossians 2:12
3. See Matthew 11:25
4. See 1 Peter 2:23
5. See Philippians 4:4
6. See John 14:9
7. John 1:26
8. See Matthew 6:25–34
9. See Matthew 28:20